THOMSON COURSE TECHNOLOGY

CourseCard Microsoft Office XP

Overview

Programs

Office XP is an integrated suite of programs for document creation, communication, data management, and business information analysis. Five programs make up the core of Office XP.

- **Word:** a word processor and desktop publishing program
- **PowerPoint:** an electronic presentation program
- **Excel:** a financial spreadsheet program
- **Outlook:** an e-mail and communication program
- **Access:** a database management program

Shortcut Bar

The Shortcut Bar provides quick access to Office files, folders, and applications.

- Create a new Word document, Excel workbook, PowerPoint presentation, or Outlook e-mail message.
- Open an Office file.
- Create a new e-mail message in Outlook.
- Create a new appointment in Outlook.
- Create a new task in Outlook.
- Create a new contact in Outlook.
- Create a new journal entry in Outlook.
- Create a new note in Outlook.
- Start Word.
- Start Excel.
- Start PowerPoint.
- Start Outlook.
- Start Access.

■ **Activate the Shortcut Bar**

1. Choose **Start**, **Programs**, **Microsoft Office Tools**, **Microsoft Office Shortcut Bar**.
2. You will be prompted to specify whether you want the Shortcut Bar to start automatically whenever Windows is started.

Common menus

Many menus and commands are shared across the Office XP suite, including:

- **File** —general file commands, such as open, close, and print
- **Edit** — general editing commands, such as cut, copy, and paste
- **View** — display commands, such as normal and print view; show rulers, toolbars, and so on
- **Insert** — commands for inserting items such as pictures, textboxes, objects, and hyperlinks
- **Format** — commands for program-specific formatting options such as fonts, slide layouts, and cell formats
- **Tools** — access to spelling checkers, program options, and other items
- **Help** — access to program-specific information and Help

Task panes

All Office XP programs, except Outlook, have task panes that appear on the right side of the program window. Common task panes include:

- New
- Clipboard
- Insert Clip Art
- Basic Search
- Advanced Search

There are also unique, program-specific task panes, such as Word's Mail Merge task pane and PowerPoint's Slide Layout task pane.

New task panes

Create a new file for the current program. Word's New Document task pane is shown here.

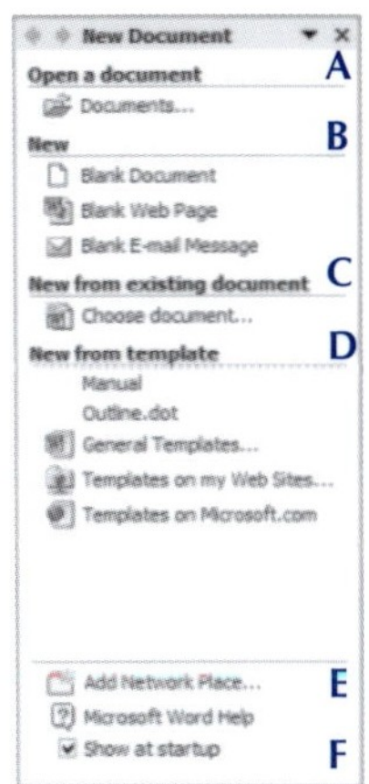

A Search for a file to open.

B Create a new file (Word document, Excel workbook, PowerPoint presentation, etc.).

C Create a new file based on an existing file.

D Create a new file from a template.

E Create and use shared folders via the Add New Network Place Wizard.

F Show or hide the task pane at startup.

Clipboard task pane

Copy multiple items (up to 24) from different programs, and then paste these items into any Office file.

A Paste all Clipboard items simultaneously at the insertion point.

B Delete all items from the Clipboard.

C A Word data item ready to be pasted into a file.

D An Excel data item ready to be pasted into a file.

E A PowerPoint data item ready to be pasted into a file.

F Turn Office Clipboard command options on or off.

Insert Clip Art task pane

Quickly find photographs, drawings, music, and other media files to use in Office documents.

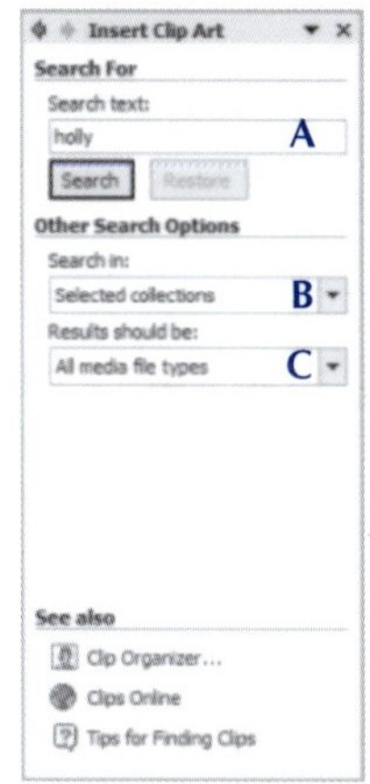

A Enter one or more keywords that describe the clip art file you're looking for.

B Specify at least one search location. You can search across multiple folders or network places.

C Specify the file type. You can search for several types of files:
- Clip art
- Photographs
- Sounds
- Movies

Basic Search task pane

Perform keyword searches of entire files and specify where you want to search.

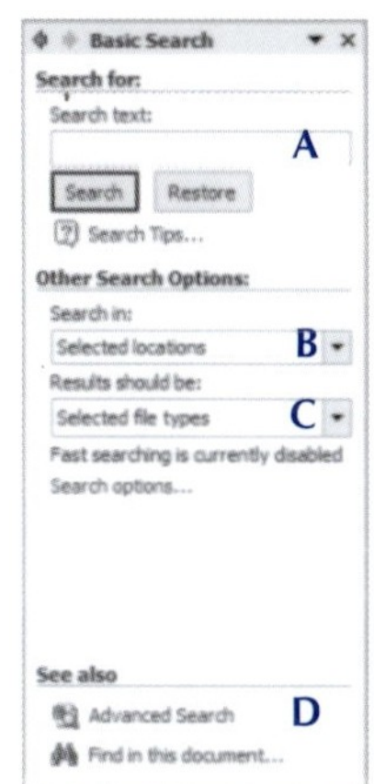

A Enter one or more words. Files containing these words are returned.

B Specify at least one search location. You can search across multiple folders or network places.

C Specify the file type, if desired. You can search for several types of files:
- Office files
- Outlook items
- Web pages

D Click to perform an Advanced Search.

Advanced Search task pane

Search by file size, file name, author, revision number, creation date, template type, and other parameters.

A Specify the file property or text type to base your search on, such as by date, file size or file name.

B Specify the condition that must be met during the search. "Includes" is the default condition.

C Enter the search value.

D Specify at least one place to search. You can search across multiple folders or network places.

E Specify the types of files you want to find.

Keyboard shortcuts

Keys	Action
F1	Display the Help window or the Office Assistant.
ALT + TAB	Switch between open programs.
CTRL + W	Close the active window.
CTRL + F6	Switch to the next program window when more than one window is active.
ALT + SHIFT + F10	Display the menu or message for a smart tag.
CTRL + F12	Open the Open dialog box.
F12	Open the Save As dialog box.
CTRL + O	Open the Open dialog box.
CTRL + P	Print a document.
CTRL + K	Insert a hyperlink.
CTRL + C	Copy the selected item to the Office Clipboard.
CTRL + X	Cut the selected item to the Office Clipboard.
CTRL + V	Paste the last copied or cut item from the Office Clipboard.

Ask a Question box

Located in the upper-right corner of all Office program windows.

- **Get Help**
  1. Type a question (or just some key words) in the Ask a Question box.

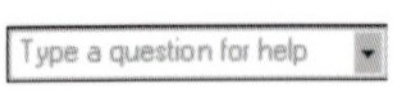

  2. Press ENTER to display a list of relevant Help topics.
  3. Click the appropriate topic to display it in the Help window.

Smart tags

Provide quick and easy access to frequently used options and commands. To work with smart tags, use one of the following three types of buttons:

- **Paste Options**
  1. Copy data from a source program.
  2. Paste the data into your destination program.
  3. Click the Paste Options smart tag button.
  4. Choose the desired formatting option from the smart tag menu.

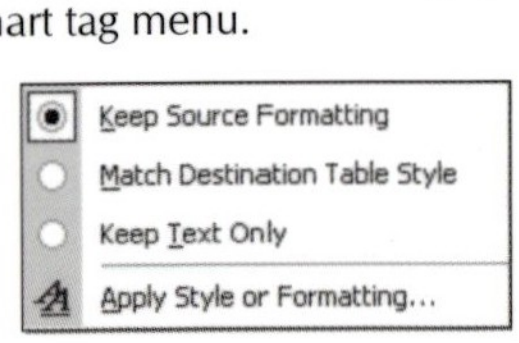

- **Smart Tag Actions**
  1. Type a name, address, or date into Word, or type a stock symbol in Excel.
  2. Recognized data is marked with a smart tag indicator (a purple dotted underline).

  3. Point to the recognized text until the Smart Tag Actions button appears.
  4. Click the button, and then choose the desired option from the smart tag menu.

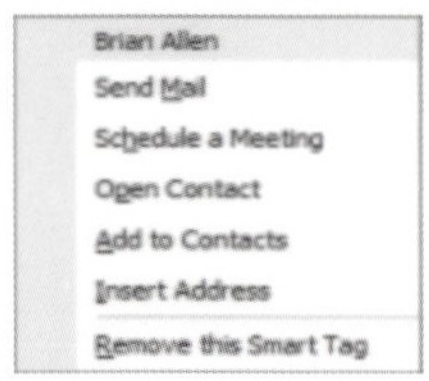

- **AutoCorrect Options**
  1. Type text that triggers an automatic correction.
  2. Point to the text that was changed automatically until the AutoCorrect Options button appears.
  3. Click the button, and then choose the desired option from the smart tag menu.

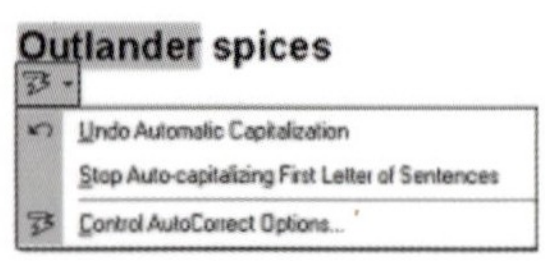

Task panes

- **Show or hide a task pane**

The task pane is displayed by default in Word, PowerPoint, Excel, and Access.

- If a task pane is closed, you can open it by choosing **View**, **Task Pane**.
- To hide the task pane in a particular Office program, clear the **Show at startup** option at the bottom of the task pane.

- **Select a task pane**

Click the arrow on the task pane window.

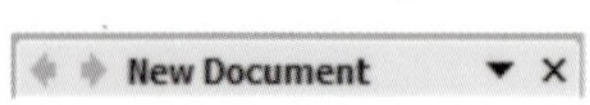

The task pane menu is divided into two sections. The top four task panes are shared across Word, PowerPoint, Excel, and Access. The bottom task panes are program-specific (Word is shown here).

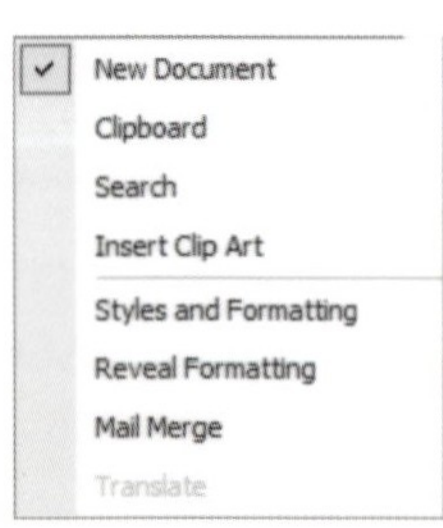

Shortcut Bar

- **Open Office files**
  1. Click the Open Office Document button.
  2. In the Open Office Document dialog box, navigate to and select the desired file(s), and then click **Open**.

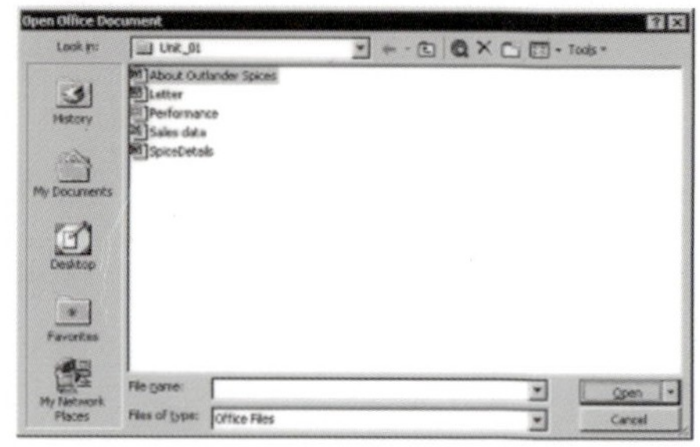

To open multiple files simultaneously, hold CTRL and select the files you want to open.

- **Create Office files**
  1. Click the New Office Document button.
  2. In the New Office Document dialog box, select the desired type of Office file.

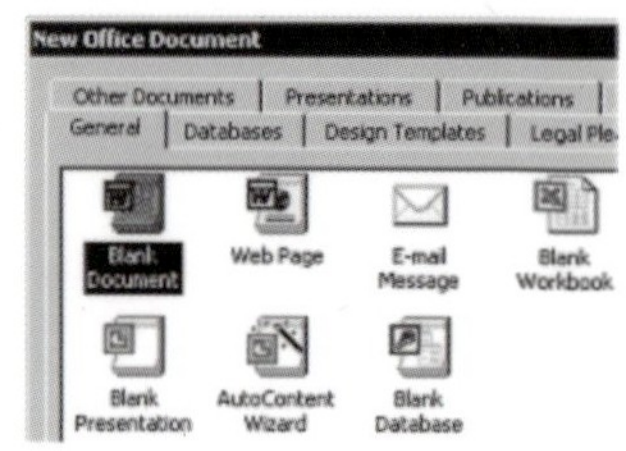

  3. Click **OK**.

Search for files

- **Search for a particular word**
  1. At the top of the task pane, click the down-arrow and select **Search**.
  2. Under Search for, in the Search text box, enter the word you want to find.
  3. Under Other Search Options, in the Search in list, verify that My Computer is checked.

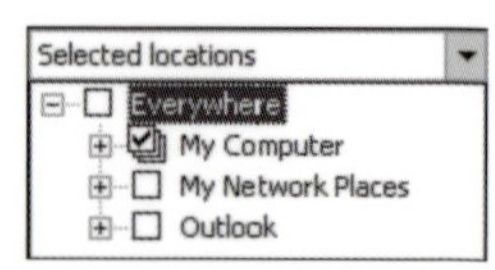

  4. Under Other Search Options, in the Results should be list, verify that Office Files is checked.

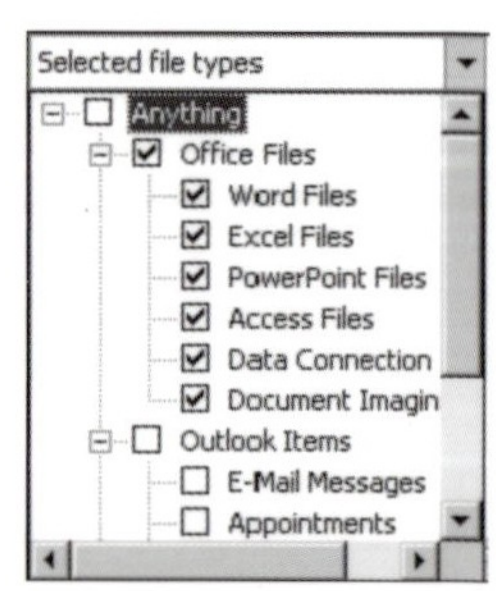

  5. Click **Search**.
  6. The Search Results task pane will display a list of Office files on your computer that contain the specified word. To open a file in its parent program, click the file name.

Sharing data

■ **Move data across programs**

1 Open the destination and source files.
2 In the source file, select the data you want to move.
3 Right-click and drag the selection to the destination file's taskbar button, but do not release the mouse button. After a moment, the destination program will be activated.
4 While continuing to hold the mouse button, drag the selection into the destination file window.
5 Release the mouse button to display the shortcut menu.
6 Choose **Move Here** to paste the selection.

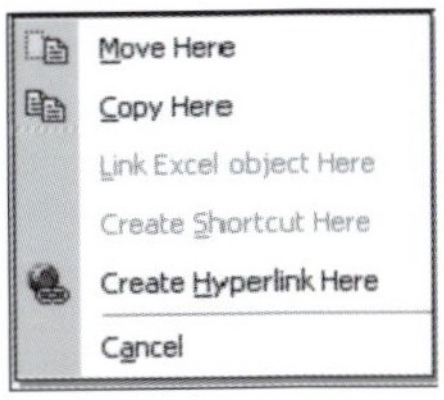

■ **Quickly copy data between programs**

1 Open the source and destination documents.
2 In the source document, select the desired text.
3 While holding CTRL, drag the selection to the destination document's taskbar button. Don't release the mouse or CTRL.
4 When the destination document appears, drop the selection in the desired location.

Linking data

A link is an active copy, or mirror, of selected data in the source file. When you create a link, any changes you make to the source file will be reflected in the destination file automatically.

■ **Create a link between two Office files**

1 Open the source and destination files.
2 Copy the source data that you want to appear in the destination file.
3 Place the insertion point where you want the linked data to appear.
4 Choose **Edit**, **Paste Special**.
5 Select **Paste link**.

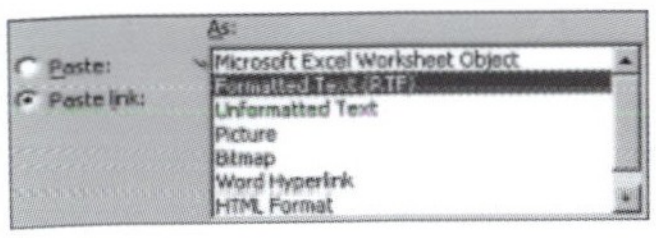

6 From the As list, select the desired format.
7 Click **OK**.

■ **Edit linked data**

1 In the destination file, right-click the linked data to display the shortcut menu.
2 Choose **Linked <format>**, **Edit Link** (where <format> is the format of the inserted data) to open the source file in its parent program.
3 Edit the data.
4 Update and close the source file.

■ **Repair a lost link**

1 Choose **Edit**, **Links**.
2 Click **Change Source**, and then select a source file from the Look in list.
3 Click **Open**.
4 In the Links dialog box, click **Update Now** to update the link.

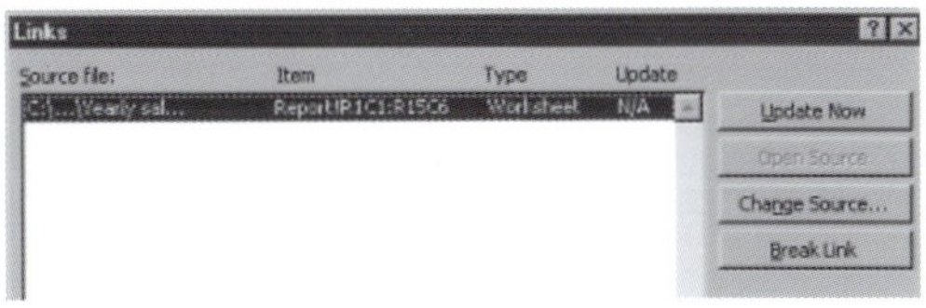

5 Click **OK**.

Hyperlinks

A hyperlink is a graphic or piece of text that you click to open another file.

■ **Create a hyperlink to another file**

1 Open the file in which you want to create the hyperlink.
2 Select the text or graphic that you want to convert into a hyperlink.
3 Choose **Insert**, **Hyperlink**.
4 In the Insert Hyperlink dialog box, navigate to and select the file you want the hyperlink to point to.

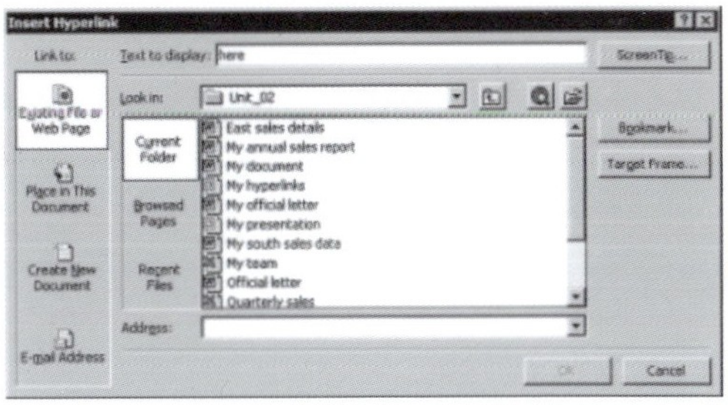

5 Click **OK** to create the hyperlink and close the Insert Hyperlink dialog box.

■ **Change the hyperlink destination**

1 Right-click the hyperlink you want to change, and then choose **Edit Hyperlink**.
2 Enter a new destination address for the hyperlink.
3 Click **OK**.

■ **Convert a hyperlink to regular text**

1 Right-click the hyperlink you want to remove, and then choose **Remove Hyperlink**.
2 Click **OK**.

Working with objects

■ **Insert clip art**

1 Place the insertion point at the desired location.
2 Choose **Insert**, **Picture**, **Clip Art**.
3 On the Insert Clip Art task pane, in the Search text box, enter a keyword.
4 Click **Search**.
5 Click the clip you want to insert.

■ **Insert a diagram**

1 Choose **Insert**, **Diagram**.
2 Click one of the following diagram types:

- **Organization Chart** — hierarchical relationships among members of an organization
- **Cycle** — steps in a continuous process
- **Radial** — relationship of a core process element to other process elements
- **Pyramid** — foundation-based relationships for a process
- **Venn** — area of overlap between and among elements of a process
- **Target** — steps leading to a goal

3 Click **OK**.
4 Do one or more of the following:
   - To add text to an element in the diagram, right-click the element, choose **Edit Text**, and then type the text.
   - To add an element, click **Insert Shape** on the Diagram toolbar.
   - To add a preset design scheme, click **AutoFormat** on the Diagram toolbar, and then select a style from the Diagram Style Gallery.
5 To finish, click outside the diagram.

■ **Insert WordArt**

1 Choose **Insert**, **Picture**, **WordArt**.
2 In the WordArt Gallery dialog box, select a WordArt style, and then click **OK**.
3 In the Edit WordArt Text dialog box, type the desired text.
4 If necessary, modify the selected WordArt style by using the Font and Size lists and the Bold and Italics buttons.
5 Click **OK**.

■ **Create a new embedded or linked object**

1 Place the insertion point where you want the linked or embedded object to appear.
2 Choose **Insert**, **Object**.
3 Click **Create from file**.
4 In the File box, type the path of the item to be embedded or linked, or click **Browse** to select the item by navigating your file system.

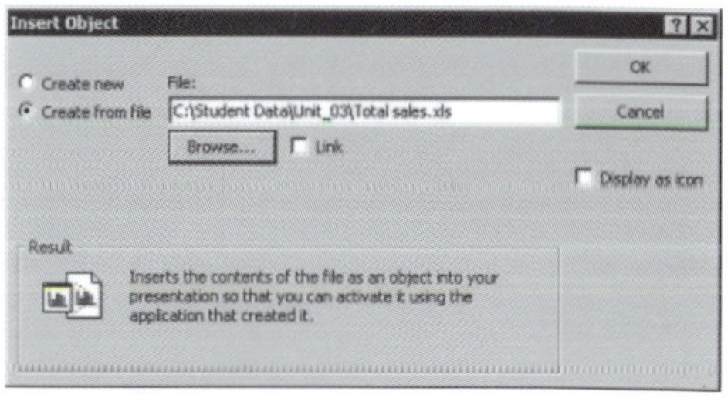

5 To create a linked object, check **Link**. If you don't check this option, an embedded object will be created.
6 To display the object as an icon, check **Display as icon**.
7 Click **OK**.

Top Productivity Tips and Solutions

1 Getting more help with Office XP. The following Web pages contain many links to useful resources:
www.microsoft.com/office
www.microsoft.com/office/support/default.asp

- Free installation support (425) 635-7056.
- Paid technical support (800) 936-5700.

2 Recovering work after a crash.
When an Office program is opened after closing prematurely, files not properly saved will appear in a Document Recovery task pane. To recover a file:

1. Click the drop-down arrow for the file you want to recover.
2. Choose **Save As**.
3. Locate and select the original file, or specify a new name and location
4. Click **Save**.

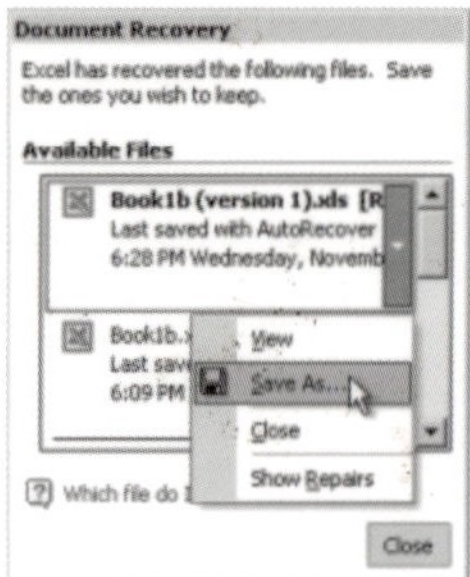

3 Save your Office settings. You can use an Office configuration file to quickly configure Office on another computer.

1. Choose **Start**, **Programs**, **Microsoft Office Tools**, **Save My Settings Wizard**, and then click **Next**.
2. Verify that Save the settings from this Machine is selected, and then click **Next**.
3. Select **Save the settings to a File**.
4. Click **Finish** to save your settings to the specified file.

4 Send Office files for review as e-mail attachments.

1. Open the file you want to send.
2. Choose **File**, **Send To**, **Mail Recipient (for Review)**.
3. In the To box, enter the reviewer's e-mail address.
4. Click **Send**.

By default, the subject line reads, "Please review '<file name>'." In the message body, the phrase "Please review the attached document" is inserted automatically.

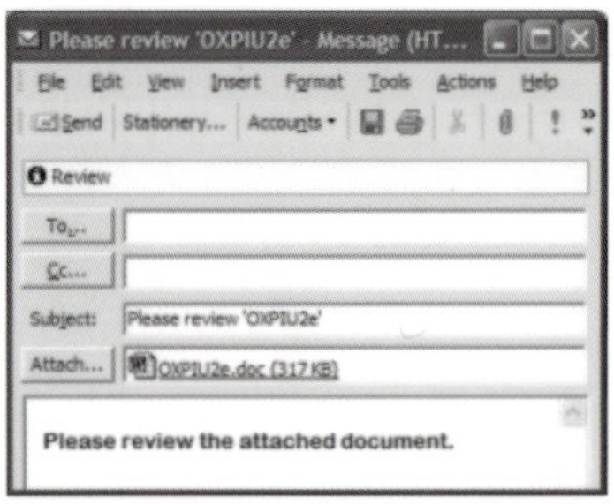

5 Send an e-mail message with an introduction. Include the contents of the current file in the body of your message.

1. Open the Office file that you want to send in the body of an e-mail message.
2. Choose **File**, **Send To**, **Mail Recipient**.

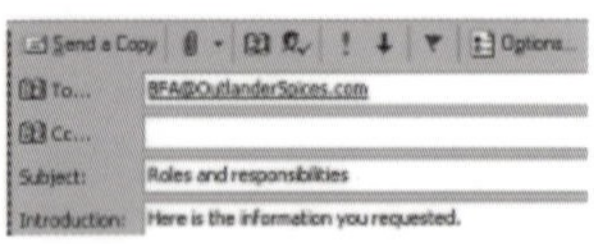

3. Enter the recipients' e-mail addresses in the To and Cc boxes.
4. Enter the desired text in the Introduction box. This text will appear at the beginning of the message.
5. In Word, click **Send a Copy**. In Excel, click **Send this Sheet**. In PowerPoint, click **Send this Slide**.
6. If Outlook is closed, start Outlook in order to transmit the message.

6 Add new clips to the Clip Organizer.

1. In the Insert Clip Art task pane, click **Clip Organizer**.
2. Choose **File**, **Add Clips to Organizer**, **Automatically**.
3. Click **OK**.

7 Compress pictures to reduc

1. Choose **View**, **Toolbars**
2. Click the Compress Pictur
3. Click **OK**.

8 Customize the Shortcut Bar You can customize the Shortcut Bar for improved functionality.

Move and resize the Shortcut Bar

1. Drag the Shortcut Bar to the top of the screen.
2. Right-click the Shortcut Bar and choose **Customize** from the shortcut menu.
3. Check **Auto Fit into Title Bar area**.

Add a toolbar to the Shortcut Bar

1. Activate the Toolbars tab.
2. In the Show these Folders as Toolbars list, check the toolbar you want to add.

Add a button to the Shortcut Bar

1. Activate the Buttons tab.
2. In the Show these Files as Buttons list, check the item you want to add to the toolbar as a button.
3. Click **OK**.

9 Change AutoCorrect items.

1. Choose **Tools**, **AutoCorrect** to open the AutoCorrect dialog box.
2. Activate the Smart Tags tab.
3. Under Recognizers, check those items that you want the program to recognize automatically (the available options will vary between programs).
4. Click **OK**.

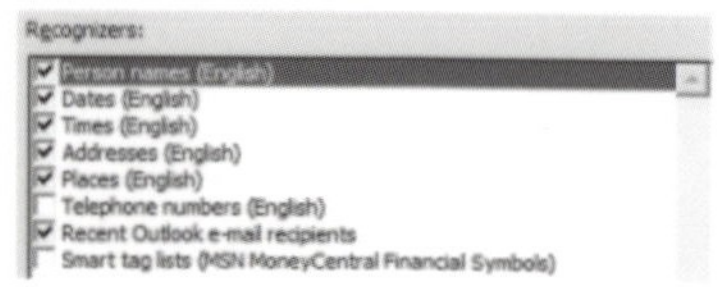

10 Publish an Office file as a Web page

1. Open the file you want to publish as a Web page.
2. Choose **File**, **Save As Web Page**.
3. Click **Publish**
4. Under Publish what, specify how much of the file should be published.
5. Under Browser support, select the browser(s) that should be supported.
6. Under Publish a copy as, in the File name box, enter the complete path for the Web page.
7. Click **Publish**.

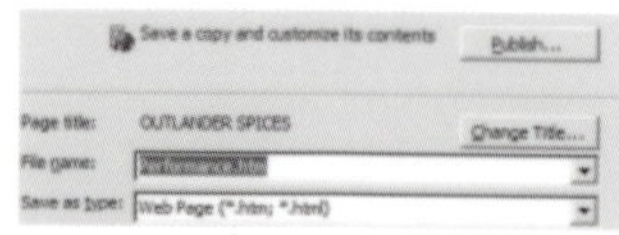

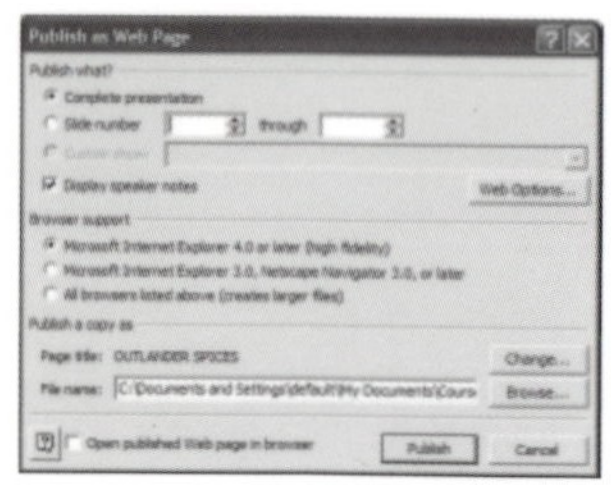

11 Use Web Queries in Excel. Easily access, analyze, and refresh data from the Web, such as stock information.

1. Go to any Web site and copy the information you want to analyze.
2. Paste the information into Excel.
3. Click the Paste Options smart tag button.
4. Choose **Create Refreshable Web Query**.
5. Select the table you want to import and click **Import**.

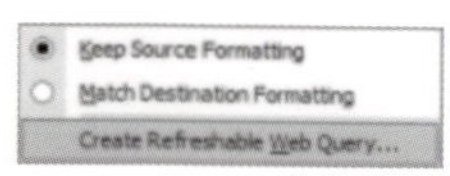

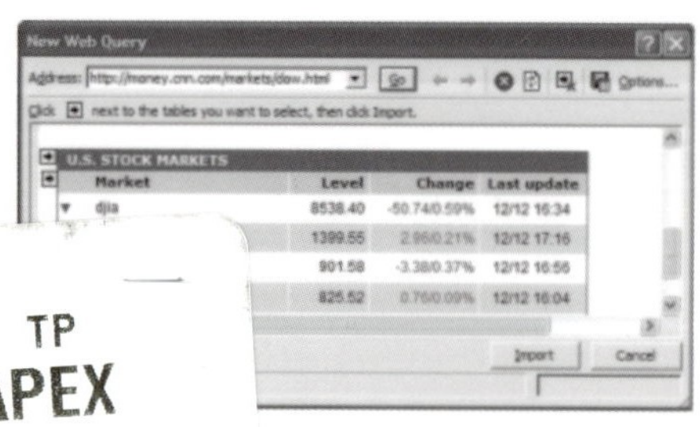

TP
APEX
9780619206192
90000>
9 780619 206192
ISBN 0-619-20619-5